ISBN: 1-4196-9687-4
ISBN-13: 9781419696879

Visit www.booksurge.com to order additional copies.

WHAT CAN CHIEF EXECUTIVES LEARN FROM STAND-UP COMEDIANS?

Fifty essential skills top performers perfect and you can learn

Roger Edward Jones

Praise for ***What Can Chief Executives Learn From Stand-up Comedians?***

"This book contains clear and memorable insights that will definitely help you improve your leadership communication skills and success in business."

— Ian Morrice
Group Chief Executive
The Warehouse Group

"Read this imaginative and practical guide if you strive to be more effective in business."

— Jim Henderson
President and CEO
Apriso

"A simple and powerful guide packed with useful tips. I recommend it to any manager who wants to climb the corporate ladder."

— Stephen Harvey
Co-founder & Chief Operating Officer
Talent Intelligence

To Juliana and our daughter, Isabella.

A special thanks to the chief executives
from France, Holland, United Kingdom
and the USA who attended my very first
*What can Chief Executives Learn From
Stand-up Comedians?*
event in Geneva, Switzerland.

Your encouraging feedback sparked
the idea to write this book.

Dear Reader

(or potential reader if you are browsing through this book online or in a bookstore),

"What can chief executives learn from stand-up comedians?"

Now there's a serious question.

When you think how chief executives refine their skills, most people list the courses they attended at prestigious business schools, executive briefings where they networked with well-known management gurus and their peers, or the executive coaches they often employ.

Well, all of these approaches are extremely valuable.

But what can chief executives learn from top-performing stand-up comedians? Comedians like Bill Hicks, Richard Pryor, Jerry Seinfeld, Chris Rock, Eddie Izzard, and Jack Dee.

I have always thought top-performing stand-up comedians are excellent communicators and have often wondered what skills and techniques they use to successfully deliver their routines. So, I decided to research and study exactly what they do to be successful. I watched hours of videos and attended comedy clubs, large and small. Then to put it all to the test I wrote and, with "butterflies in my stomach," delivered a stand-up comedy routine. And to make sure I didn't back out at the last minute I invited thirty of my corporate clients to see me perform...and guess what—they all attended! Well, I'm pleased to say I really enjoyed the experience at a comedy club in London (though I have no plans to give up my "day job"!).

Importantly, I now realize that chief executives (and indeed all of us in business) can learn a lot from these great stand-up comedy performers.

In this book you will discover fifty techniques used by top performing stand-up comedians. Reflect on the thoughts and questions I share with you and you might, just might, start to become even more effective in your day-to-day business life.

1.
Preparation

Good stand-up comedians' performances
appear totally spontaneous, almost
as if they have just walked into the venue
and are talking "off-the-cuff."
The reality is quite different.
They spend hours and hours honing their
material and practicing their routines.

Do you spend a sufficient amount of time
preparing for your conference speeches
and client meetings?

2.
Less Is More

A comic's messages or jokes aren't typically long-winded, but tight and well crafted. They are designed to get their message across with precision focus.

How can you deliver your key messages using fewer words?

3.
Opinion

Stand-up comedians aren't "gray"'
people who never express their points
of view. They do not hesitate to
give their opinions.

Do you effectively contribute to business meetings by expressing your opinions?

4.
Stories

Stand-up comedians don't use bullet points to deliver their messages; instead they use stories. Their stories engage audiences on an emotional level and are remembered.

Are you currently using stories to bring your messages to life?

5.

Role Models

Many comics invest time to study the skills and approaches of their peers at the top of their fields. They want to constantly "up their game."

Who are your role models and what can you learn from them?

6.
Originality

Comics don't plagiarize their material from others. Instead they work hard to produce original material that bears their trademarks.

Can you be more original in your approach to leadership?

7.
Perspective

Comics see even the most mundane things in a different way. This helps spark ideas as they write their material.

How can you enhance your problem-solving skills by seeing things from a different perspective?

8.
Simplicity

Although a stand-up comic will sometimes tell a long, convoluted story, the message it delivers will typically be crystal clear and simple.

Although business can be complex, can you simplify some of the messages you need to put across?

9.

Analogies

Listen to how comics use analogies to explain and reinforce their material.

What analogies could you use to help explain your important messages?

10.
Test

Before doing a big "gig" comedians will often test their material on smaller audiences and fine-tune their routines accordingly.

Is there someone you can ask to give you feedback on your messages before you deliver them to key stakeholders?

11.
Comfort Zone

Stand-up comics will experiment and try new material or deliver existing material in a different way. They won't stay in their comfort zone but instead will constantly challenge themselves.

What can you do to expand your comfort zone?

12.
Engagement

Comics' number one concern is to hook the audience in the first few seconds. If they don't, they are highly likely to "bomb."

How can you hook people with your messages in the first few seconds?

13.
Confidence

Although comedians may have "the butterflies" when they walk out to perform, they will project a sense of confidence.

What impression do you leave with people when they meet you?

14.
Personalization

When you visit comedy clubs you may not realize it but you are being watched. The comics will observe the audience to get a sense of the atmosphere and mix of people. They will then aim to personalize parts of their routines.

Do you personalize your messages to the various business audiences (internal and external) you speak to?

15.
The Heckler

Stand-up comedians always have answers when they are heckled.

Do you always have answers prepared for the questions you might be asked about your propositions?

16.
Revelation

Comics will often reveal details of their own day-to-day lives.

Could you reveal a little more about yourself to appear less remote from those who work for you?

17.
Show

All comedians want to put on a good "show."

Can you put on a better "show" in your presentations and meetings and make them a little more interesting by moving away from the standard agendas?

18.

Self-deprecation

Although comedians take their profession very seriously they will not hesitate to use self-deprecating humor to help their audiences identify with them.

Could you benefit from using a little self-deprecation from time to time to help others identify with you?

19.
Voice Variety

Listen to how comics use their voices to engage. They pause, whisper, speed up, and even change the tone of their voices.

How can you make your voice more engaging and less monotone?

20.
Technology

The only technology stand-up comedians use to deliver their routines is a microphone. They don't use fancy graphics and hundreds of PowerPoint slides.

Could you deliver your next conference speech without using PowerPoint slides?

21. Improvisation

Good comics are masters of the art of improvisation. If a calamity strikes when they are delivering their routines they make it appear that it was meant to happen.

What disaster recovery plan do you have in place should the unexpected happen?

22.
Feedback

The true test of comics' material is feedback from the audience. This helps fine-tune their routines and "up" their performances.

Can you put in place a feedback mechanism so you can improve your leadership skills?

23. Ambiguity

Some comics are very comfortable going off into their own world as they deliver their material with highly amusing but sometimes very ambiguous stories of everyday life.

Are you comfortable with some ambiguity in your business life or do you prefer to operate by hard-and-fast rules?

24. Body Language

Comics don't (or at least most of them don't) stand up in front of audiences motionless as they deliver their routines. They know that effectively using their body language enhances their performances.

Do you just stand up in front of audiences like a cardboard cutout or are you animated as you deliver your talks?

25.
The Turn up

Just having the courage to turn up and deliver a comedy routine can be a great personal achievement (as I know from experience!).

Do you ever avoid situations that might make you feel uncomfortable?

26.
Small Talk

Many comedians don't just jump headlong into their routines. Instead they will engage some of the audience in small talk to warm them up and find out a bit about them.

Do you use small talk to engage and find out a little bit about your clients and team members?

27.
Humor for All

The humor of many comics appeals to all, whether they are chief executives or shop floor workers.

Do your messages appeal to all your various audiences or just to those you are most comfortable with?

28.
Self-belief

Great stand-up comedians believe they will succeed. This self-belief helps ensure they perform well.

Do your self-beliefs support or undermine your performance?

29.

Enjoyment

When you watch most comics they look as if they are enjoying themselves rather than as if they are standing in front of their audience as some sort of punishment.

Do you look as if you enjoy your job when you interact with your customers, staff, or shareholders?

30.
No Judgment

Few comics are judgmental about their audiences or other people in their routines.

Do you suspend judgment at times and accept people for who they are?

31.
Big Break

Many up-and-coming comics look for opportunities to get a big break. Maybe this is a TV appearance or winning a competition. It is the thing that will help skyrocket them to success.

What can you do to help skyrocket yourself to success? Learn a new skill? Play to your strengths? Network more?

32.

The Face-to-Face

Comics know that the best way to perform is face-to-face in front of an audience, not by sending brief impersonal e-mails.

Are there times when it would be more effective to have a face-to-face meeting rather than fire off a brief e-mail from your cell phone?

33.
Radar

It is almost as if a comic has an internal radar system. Based on the reaction of the audience, a comic often adapts a routine while delivering it.

Do you have opportunities to be more observant and more sensitive to the reactions of those around you in meetings?

34.
Self-awareness

To make it to the top of their game comedians must be fully aware of their impact on audiences.

How many marks out of ten would you award yourself for self-awareness?

35.
Writing Buddy

Writing material alone can at times be easy but sometimes a comic hits a blockage. A writing buddy can help a comic spark ideas for new material.

Is there someone you could work with to add some sparkle and new dimensions to your pitches?

36.
Career Plan

Most comics have a career plan—they want to progress from "open mic" slots to twenty-minute performances to forty-five-minute slots and then go on tour. After that they could be lucky enough to appear on TV.

Have you developed a well-defined career plan for the next five, ten, twenty years?

37.
Timing

Comics deliver their punch lines with precision timing for maximum impact. Timing is key for their success.

Could you manage and prioritize your time more effectively so key tasks and deadlines don't slip?

38.
Risk

Every now and then a comic will take a big risk with material or delivery style and perhaps include something that is a little close to the edge.

Is there a (calculated) risk you could take to set you apart from your competition?

39.

Persistence

Few comics become overnight successes. They need to persist even when audiences are tough and new routines don't quite work as well as they hoped.

Are you being persistent enough in your endeavors or are you giving up just a little too soon?

40.
Conversation

Comics don't stand in front of their audiences and lecture them; instead they have a conversational style.

When you stand up in front of audiences do you adopt a lecturing or conversational delivery style?

41.
Repetition

Listen to how some comics repeat certain lines and phrases to spark laughter. The audience will often remember these repeated lines long after the show has finished.

Are you repeating your key messages so people remember them?

42.
Silence

As good comics tell their stories you can often hear a pin drop as they use the power of silence to create a sense of intrigue and suspense.

Could you use the power of silence a little more when negotiating?

43.

Respect Time

Comics will often have to deliver their routines within strict time limits.

Do you sometimes ramble on way beyond your allocated time limit at meetings and when giving presentations?

44.
Change Style

Experienced comics can change their style depending on the makeup of an audience and even adapt their material accordingly.

Can you effectively change your leadership style to suit the people you are with and the situation?

45.
Gut Feel

Sometimes the test for new material is simply whether it feels right. It's about trusting your intuition.

Do you use your intuition to make decisions in business?

46.
Consistency

Good comics won't just turn up and "wing it." Instead they will aim to be consistent and give their best at every performance.

Do you consistently give your best or do you sometimes lose interest?

47.
Humor

Well, it is a "glimpse of the obvious" but stand-up comedians are funny. Appropriate humor, well delivered at the right time, can be powerful for both breaking the ice and getting a message remembered.

Is a little humor something you could integrate into your repertoire?

48.
Performance

Some comics will monitor their performances and even work out how many laughs they get per minute of material. They then tweak their routines to increase the amount of laughter they receive.

What performance criteria can you put in place for yourself?

49. Responsibility

When comics "bomb" in front of an audience they know it is their fault. They take full responsibility.

Do you always take full responsibility for your actions?

50.
Brand

Comedians work hard to develop their own unique identities–something that sets them apart from the crowd.

What sets you apart from the crowd?

About the author:

Roger Edward Jones is one of Europe's foremost leadership experts. He has delivered speeches and seminars to thousands of people across Europe, Asia and the USA.

Roger believes that each person has extraordinary untapped potential that he or she can learn to access and, in so doing, achieve their true potential and make a greater contribution to their organization.

Roger is a dynamic conference speaker known for his insightful and powerful storytelling. He is also a sought-after seminar leader, executive coach and bestselling author. His clients include many Fortune 500 firms. Roger's work has been featured in the international business press and on the BBC.

Prior to establishing his business, Roger's career spanned over twenty years in blue-chip firms in the oil, finance, technology, and service sectors. He possesses an MBA degree from Cranfield School of Management and BSc and MSc degrees in science subjects.

He lives in London, UK and works worldwide.

For free resources and information about Roger's conference speeches, seminars and coaching programs visit: www.RogerEdwardJones.com

CPSIA information can be obtained at www.ICGtesting.com
262757BV00007B/8/P

9 781419 696879